The Day it Rained Iguanas

by Lauren Darnell

illustrated by K. Rose

To Lucy

 Title/The Day It Rained Iguanas/written by Lauren Darnell & illustrated by K. Rose | Edition 2
ISBN: 9780578741901 Imprint: Independently published Audience ages 4-8 | Summary:Maria is terrified of reptiles, but she won't let that stop her from saving the iguanas raining from the sky | SUBJECTS: Overcoming fear-Fiction | Friendship-Fiction | Environmental protection-Fiction |

This book is dedicated in memory of my Nannie, Oralee McCaig who taught me to daydream without restraint and who would have been happy this wasn't a book about a rat.

Living in Florida can be tough for someone like me who's scared of reptiles.
We have alligators in the swamps, snakes in the grass,
turtles in the ponds, and worst of all LIZARDS!

Lizards are anywhere the other reptiles hang out
and everywhere the others can't be.

They'll sit on rocks when I go out to play, stick to the door
when I want to come inside, and hide in the grass
until I walk past to run over my toes!

Florida has big lizards, small lizards, green lizards, red lizards, fat lizards, fast lizards, jumping lizards, and even lizards that change color. Too many to count, but I do my best to avoid them all!

Everything changed one winter morning when I woke up to a chill in the air. Cold days are rare in Florida, but that wasn't keeping me inside on a Saturday. That would take an alligator!

"Not so fast Maria. You'll freeze if you go out in that today," Mama called from the kitchen before I could run out the door.

Back in my room, I put on a long sleeved shirt, a jacket, traded my favorite rainbow flip-flops out for my rain boots and added a tutu for style.

After adding a hat, Mama gave my new layered look a nod of approval and sent me out to play. I was out the back door as fast as I could before she added anything else to my outfit.

It was too cold to play mermaids in the pool, so my choices were clearly lemonade stand or bug hospital. I jumped off the porch to get started, but a gust of wind knocked me over.

I got back to my feet, but the wind was still making me toss and tumble all over the yard.

Even the palm trees rattled and danced in time with the gusts.

The wind was so hard it made something fall right out of the tree. Something big. It landed on the ground with a great, big SPLAT!

"MMMAAAMMMMAAAAA!"

It was the worst thing that had ever happened!

It was horrible!

It was terrible!

It wasn't moving?

Something was wrong.

Lizards are fast. Usually by the time I knew I had seen one they were gone in a flash. I inched a bit closer to check on the thing, ready to run and ready to scream, but the closer I got the longer he stayed.

That's when I noticed it was upside down. I reached out a hand, squeezed my eyes closed tight, and before I could change my mind, I flipped the iguana back over like a pancake. I thought that would fix it, but still it didn't move.

It looked like it was just sleeping, but I had never seen anything so sleepy that it fell out of a tree before.

Up close the iguana wasn't as scary as I thought it would be. In fact, it was kind of cute, and I decided it needed help.

Putting him back in the tree was out of the question but I couldn't just leave it outside in the cold. I crept through the house and up to my room to find a warm place to put it down.

If I had just fallen asleep I would want to be tucked into a soft, warm bed. Even though I wasn't as scared anymore I wasn't ready to share MY bed, so I put it down to rest in my doll's bed instead.

I wondered what iguanas like to eat and if they like tea parties when I heard my name being called from the living room.

Uh-oh...

"Look here, the news says lizards are falling out of trees all over town," Mama said.

"Will the iguanas be ok?" I asked.

"Maybe if someone comes along to help them. but they just can't be in this cold too long," Mama said.

"Can I go out to play still?" I asked.

"If you are sure you still want to. Watch for falling iguanas!" Mama said, as she picked back up her book.

"I will!" I promised her over my shoulder.

Mama was right. Someone needed to help the iguanas.
If that someone was going to be me, I would need some gear first.

I borrowed two oven mitts to protect me from their claws, a bike helmet to protect me from their falls, and a crawfish net to protect the iguanas from gravity!

Even from the front yard I could see the news was right.
There were iguanas raining down all over, and I was going to catch them all.

It was a good thing I had a net ready. I caught one iguana falling off the roof next door, two more sliding down from the trees in our front yard, and another coming off an umbrella by the pool.

Soon my net was full, but so was my room.
There were still more iguanas to catch, so I was going to have to find somewhere else to put them to warm up.

On my next trip back inside, I put one in the flowerpot, another in my slippers, a few in the towel closet, and a big one in the desk drawer.

I tucked them in anywhere I could while Mama read her book, but after I filled up the bathtub with iguanas I was REALLY out of room.

I came home exhausted, but sure I had rescued every cold-stunned iguana in the neighborhood. There was no time to rest though, as I came home to a whole new problem....

A house full of iguanas! They were warm, awake, and running around everywhere.

"MAAARRRIIIAA! Why are there lizards in my kitchen?" Mama shouted from on top of the chair.

"I helped them warm up, just like you said," I explained to her as an iguana crawled over my feet.

"Now we need help," Mama said, putting her phone to her ear.

Mama called for an animal expert to come wrangle all the lizards. He caught them all over the house almost as fast as I did the first time and stacked them up in crates in his van to relocate them.

Well, all of them except for the one still
snoozing away in my doll's bed.

"Can we please keep him?" I asked.

"Fine Maria, but he's got to stay
out of my kitchen, "Mama agreed with a sigh.

Since that day we've lived happily ever after with Verde the green iguana, and lizards don't scare me anymore.

KICKSTARTER

The Day It Rained Iguanas was made entirely possible by the community behind this project and the early backers who believed in it. Thank you so much for your kind words, support, and willingness to back this project. I hoped you enjoyed it as much as you thought you would the first time that you saw Maria & Verde posing for the promo images and that this book will become a favorite in your library for years to come. We sincerely couldn't have made this book without all of your help, but there are a few people who were extra generous in their donation to make sure our goal was met. For that we would like to extend a special thank you to the following people:

Deanna & JJ Boese ,Tim, Jennifer, & Colby Darnell
Jonathan & Judi Grady, Elizabeth Vaughan, Adalyn McIntosh
Jason, Gabriel, Alexander, & Liam Arndt
Ed & Pearl Brown, Kristi McCaig , Sean "McSeanold" Demer Joanna Loudamy , Tinker Green
Amy & David Shugart, Kevin & Patricia Clarke,
Eddie Lee Harbour & Aunt Becka

Finally a special thanks to all of our littlest fans for sending in art work and fan projects to celebrate the launch of the book. Never stop creating and remember to watch to falling iguanas!

Art made by: (First Row) Chloe age 9, Anna age 10, Dawsyn age 12, (Second Row) Karson age 8, Logan age 6 , & Gavin age 5.

Lauren Darnell- Author

Lauren Darnell is a children's literature author that lives and works in West Texas. Writing was her childhood dream and reading is a passion she has passed down to her two beautiful children Gavin & Lynnlee. The Day It Rained Iguanas is Lauren's 11th picture book and she got the idea after watching the news coverage of the same real life phenomenon happening in Florida. When she isn't lost in make believe worlds, Lauren loves playing with her children, reading, doing puzzles, and watching anime with her husband Adam.

K. Rose- Illustrator

K. Rose is a freelance illustrator working out of the greater Boston Area. She creates all her work from her home studio with feline assistant, Coco. K got her start creating and selling her own work around her local comic scene, and now creates work for children's media, graphic novels, and webcomics. When she isn't working, K enjoys reading, baking, and the occasional 10-hour D&D game

Made in the USA
Columbia, SC
25 September 2021

46181022R00022